Oxford
the photographic atlas

www.getmapping.com

First published in 2004 by
HarperCollins Publishers
77-85 Fulham Palace Road
London W6 8JB

The Collins website is
www.collins.co.uk

Collins is a registered trademark of HarperCollins Publishers.

Photography © 2004 Getmapping plc

Getmapping plc hereby asserts its moral right to be identified as the author
of this work.

Getmapping can produce an individual print of any area shown in this book, or of
any area within the United Kingdom. The image can be centred wherever you
choose, printed at any size from A6 to 7.5 metres square, and at any scale up to
1:1,000. For further information, please contact Getmapping on 01530 835685 or
log on to **www.getmapping.com**.

Cartography on pages reproduced by permission of
Geographer's A-Z Map Co. Ltd. Licence No. B2043
©Crown Copyright 2003. All rights reserved. Licence number 100017302

The publisher regrets that it can accept no responsibility for any errors or
omissions within this publication, or for any expense or loss thereby caused.

The representation of a road, track or footpath is not evidence of a right of way.

A CIP catalogue record for this book is available from the British Library.

ISBN 0 00 716654 0

Atlas prepared for HarperCollins Publishers by Martin Brown
Texts by Ian Harrison
Colour origination by Colourscan, Singapore
Printed and bound, by Editoriale Johnson, Italy

Previous pages: Central Oxford

contents

foreword

Oxford first grew up in the 8th century around an Augustinian priory founded by St Frideswide close to the 'ford for oxen' from which the city takes its name. Christ Church College now stands on the site of St Frideswide's – the priory was dissolved by Cardinal Wolsey and its buildings and church incorporated into what Wolsey founded as Cardinal College in 1525. The college was re-founded in 1546 after Wolsey's fall from favour and subsequent death, at which time the church was designated a cathedral and the college renamed Christ Church. Close to Magdalen Bridge is Oscar Wilde's alma mater Magdalen College, famous for the May Day hymn sung from the tower by the college choir; Magdalen's original buildings date from the late 15th century, while the so-called New Buildings were begun in 1733. Other notable colleges include: New College, founded in 1379 by William of Wykeham, Bishop of Winchester; Queen's College, built from 1672-1760 by architects including Christopher Wren; All Souls College, founded in 1438 as a memorial to soldiers killed in battles including Agincourt and Crécy; University College, Oxford's oldest, founded in 1249 by William, Archdeacon of Durham; and Merton College, founded in 1264 by Walter de Merton (later Bishop of Rochester) in Malden, Surrey – the college moved to Oxford about a decade later, where it became the model for the collegiate system. However, Oxford's most famous landmark is the Radcliffe Camera, an Italianate rotunda funded by the eminent doctor and MP John Radcliffe and built from 1737-1749 as the Radcliffe Library. It is now the main reading room of the Bodleian Library, which was reopened in 1602 by Thomas Bodley, who had spent a vast amount of money restoring and extending the 15th century library of Duke Humphrey –the Bodleian is Britain's second largest library, and is said to contain 80 miles of shelves.

places of interest within oxford city centre (pages 8-25)

city centre plan

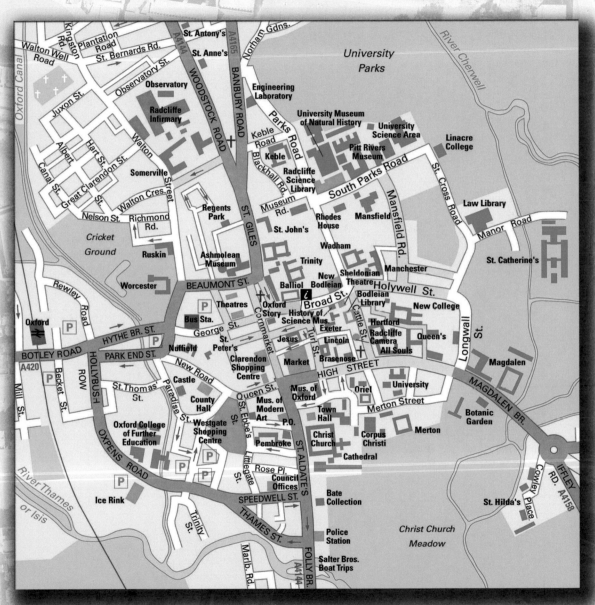

scale 1:1,562.5

1

The institution which takes up most of this picture is not a college but the Radcliffe Infirmary **(1)**. It was built from 1761-70 using funds bequeathed by Dr John Radcliffe, a Yorkshire-born physician who studied at University College (p. 19), was later elected a Fellow of Lincoln College (p. 18) and served as royal physician to William III & Queen Mary, and to their successor, Queen Anne. The Radcliffe Infirmary contains some of the specialist units of the John Radcliffe Hospital in Headington (p. 67), which is one of the country's leading teaching hospitals. Immediately to the north of the infirmary is Green College **(2)**, funded principally by Dr and Mrs Cecil Green of Texas, and founded in 1979 for Fellows and graduate students in medicine. Somerville College **(3)** was founded in 1879 as a hall for women, and was named after the Scottish mathematician Mary Somerville, who had died seven years earlier, in 1872. Alumni include two female Prime Ministers, Indira Ghandi and Margaret Thatcher, as well as Somerville's daughter, also called Mary, an educationalist and broadcaster who in 1950 became the first woman to achieve the rank of Controller at the BBC. Sandwiched between Woodstock Road and Banbury Road is the Acland Hospital **(4)**, named after former Regius Professor of Medicine Henry Acland who also championed the establishment of the University Museum (p. 12). Keble College **(5)** was founded in 1870 as a memorial to churchman and poet, the Rev. John Keble, who took a double first at Corpus Christi College (p. 23) at the age of 18, was later elected a Fellow of Oriel College (p. 18), and served as Oxford Professor of Poetry from 1831–41. Keble was also a leader of the Oxford Movement (encouraging a return to High Church ideals), the establishment of which he inspired with a 1933 sermon on national apostasy. The Oxford University Press **(6)** moved to this site in 1830 after being housed first in the Sheldonian Theatre and then in the adjacent Clarendon Building (both p. 18); Lord Clarendon's name survives in the Clarendon Press, which remains an imprint of the OUP.

scale 1:1,562.5

To the west of St Giles, the street which divides the picture, are three establishments with religious connections: St Benet's Hall **(1)**, Regent's Park College **(2)** and St Cross College **(3)**, the last of which is a relatively recent arrival from its original home further east, close to St Cross Church (p. 14). St Benet's was established in 1897 as a hall for Benedictine Monks, and became a Permanent Private Hall in 1918. Regent's Park College was established in the early 19th century close to Regent's Park in London as a training centre for Baptist ministers, moved to Oxford in 1938, and became a Permanent Private Hall in 1957. Kellogg Hall **(4)** was founded in 1990 as Oxford's 36th college, specifically for mature students on part-time degree courses. The college occupies part of Rewley House which was originally a girls' school and was converted and modernised in 1986 using money from the Kellogg Foundation, hence the name of the college. The Ashmolean Museum **(5)** is rated as 'one of the finest [museums] outside London' and dates from 1675, when the antiquary Elias Ashmole, a graduate of Brasenose College (p. 18), offered the University a collection of rarities known as the Musaeum Tradescantium or, more popularly, Tradescant's Ark. The collection was amassed by John Tradescant the Elder and his son John Tradescant the Younger, both of whom had served as head gardener to Charles I; the 'Ark' was later bequeathed to Ashmole by his friend Tradescant the Younger before Ashmole offered it to the University and the collection moved to Oxford. To the east of St Giles lies St John's College **(6)**, founded in 1555 by Sir Thomas White, a former Lord Mayor of London and a member of the Company of Merchant Taylors – the college is dedicated to and takes its name from St John the Baptist, the patron saint of taylors. Trinity College **(7)**, with its extensive gardens **(8)**, is exactly the same age as St John's, having been founded in 1555 by Sir Thomas Pope, and, like St John's, Trinity stands on the site of an earlier monastic college that was closed during Henry VIII's Dissolution of the Monasteries. Similarly, Wadham College **(9)** stands on the site of the former monastery of the Austin Friars, although Wadham was not founded until 1610, by Nicholas and Dorothy Wadham. The New Bodleian Library **(10)** was designed by Sir Giles Gilbert Scott and built from 1937–40 to house the overspill from the original Bodleian Library across the road (p.17), to which it is linked by a tunnel and conveyor belt.

1

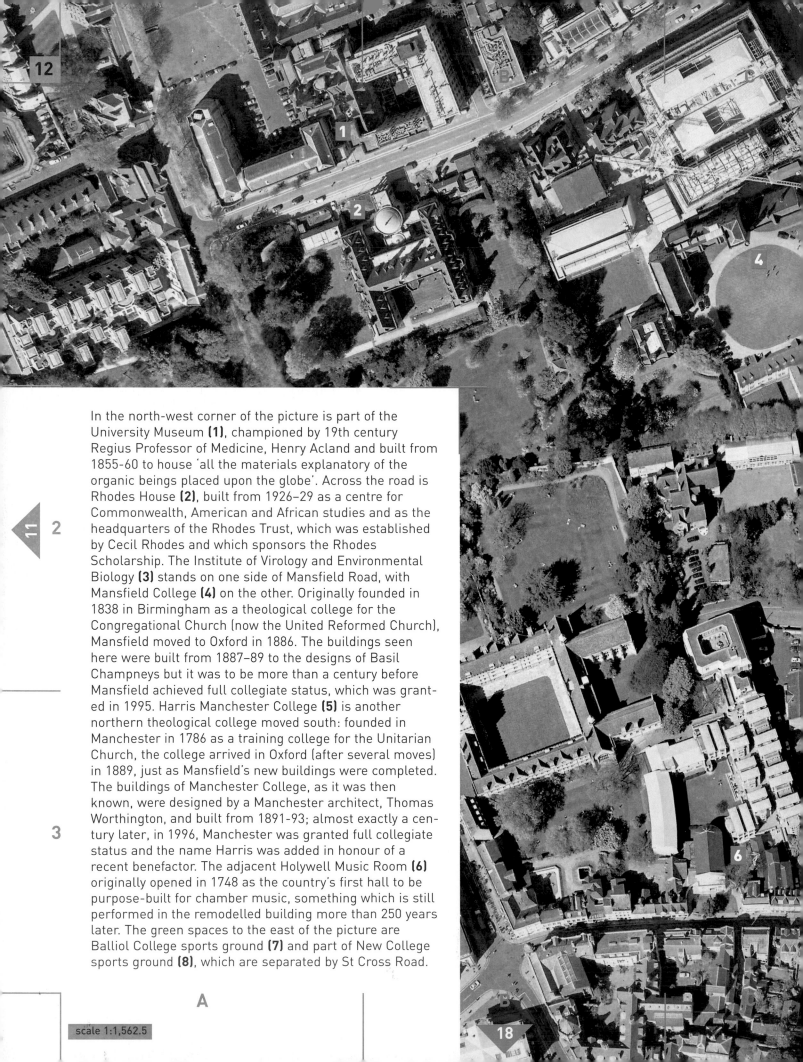

In the north-west corner of the picture is part of the University Museum **(1)**, championed by 19th century Regius Professor of Medicine, Henry Acland and built from 1855-60 to house 'all the materials explanatory of the organic beings placed upon the globe'. Across the road is Rhodes House **(2)**, built from 1926–29 as a centre for Commonwealth, American and African studies and as the headquarters of the Rhodes Trust, which was established by Cecil Rhodes and which sponsors the Rhodes Scholarship. The Institute of Virology and Environmental Biology **(3)** stands on one side of Mansfield Road, with Mansfield College **(4)** on the other. Originally founded in 1838 in Birmingham as a theological college for the Congregational Church (now the United Reformed Church), Mansfield moved to Oxford in 1886. The buildings seen here were built from 1887–89 to the designs of Basil Champneys but it was to be more than a century before Mansfield achieved full collegiate status, which was grant-ed in 1995. Harris Manchester College **(5)** is another northern theological college moved south: founded in Manchester in 1786 as a training college for the Unitarian Church, the college arrived in Oxford (after several moves) in 1889, just as Mansfield's new buildings were completed. The buildings of Manchester College, as it was then known, were designed by a Manchester architect, Thomas Worthington, and built from 1891-93; almost exactly a cen-tury later, in 1996, Manchester was granted full collegiate status and the name Harris was added in honour of a recent benefactor. The adjacent Holywell Music Room **(6)** originally opened in 1748 as the country's first hall to be purpose-built for chamber music, something which is still performed in the remodelled building more than 250 years later. The green spaces to the east of the picture are Balliol College sports ground **(7)** and part of New College sports ground **(8)**, which are separated by St Cross Road.

A

scale 1:1,562.5

1

St Catherine's College **(1)** enjoys an idyllic setting beside Holywell Mill Stream **(2)**, surrounded by the green fields of New College sports ground **(3)**, the Great Meadow **(4)**, and Merton College sports ground **(5)**. The modern architecture of St Catherine's, with its open courtyard, is a great contrast to the traditional enclosed quads and red brick cloisters of Oxford's medieval colleges. St Catherine's began life in 1868 as a society for non-collegiate students and achieved collegiate status in 1963 when work on these new buildings was well under way. They were built from 1960-64, using pre-cast concrete and specially made yellow brick, to the designs of Danish architect, Arne Jacobsen, an exponent of the International Modern style championed by Frank Lloyd Wright, Walter Gropius, Mies van der Rohe and Le Corbusier. To the north of Manor Road is the St Cross Building **(6)**, home of the English and Law Faculties and their libraries, which was built from 1961-64, at the same time as St Catherine's, to the designs of Leslie Martin and Colin Wilson. Martin was a Professor of Architecture at Cambridge University, and his work includes Caius College, Cambridge (also designed with Wilson), and College Hall at Leicester University. Across the road from the St Cross Building are Holywell Manor **(7)** and St Cross Church and cemetery, with the original home of St Cross College **(8)** to the south; the college is now situated on St Giles (p. 10). Close to the church is the holy well after which the parish is named, and which also gives its name to Holywell Mill Stream **(2)**, a branch of the Cherwell. The chuchyard is the last resting place of author Kenneth Grahame (The Wind in the Willows), theatre critic Kenneth Tynan, and shopkeeper Theophilus Carter, who was said to be Lewis Carroll's inspiration for the Mad Hatter in Alice in Wonderland.

scale 1:1,562.5

E

Town meets gown in this photograph, which includes landmark public buildings, markets ancient and modern, and four colleges. For shopping, there is the modern Clarendon Shopping Centre **(1)** or the more traditional covered market **(2),** whose façade dates from 1774. This area is also home to No. 3 Cornmarket Street **(3)**, formerly the Crown Tavern (where Shakespeare often stayed), and now famous for the 16th century wall paintings in the appropriately named Painted Room. 'Town' buildings include the Apollo Theatre **(4)**, which stages opera, ballet, musicals and pantomime, the Oxford Story **(5)**, which provides a pictorial history of the university. The Town Hall **(6)** was built from 1893-97 and, as well as its civic function, also houses the Museum of Oxford, with exhibits on the history of the city, as opposed to simply the university. Carfax was the heart of ancient Oxford, being the junction of roads arriving from the four points of the compass – now High Street, St Aldate's, Cornmarket Street and Queen Street. The name Carfax derives either from the Latin quadrifurcus, meaning 'four forks', or from the French quatre vois, meaning 'four ways', but it is synonymous with St Martin's Tower **(7)**, (often referred to as Carfax Tower). The tower is the only surviving part of the 14th century St Martin's Church, the rest of which was demolished in 1896. St Peter's College **(8)** began life in 1928 as a Private Hall for Church of England ordinands, and was granted full collegiate status in 1961. The idea of such a Hall was initiated by F.J. Chavasse, Bishop of Liverpool, and St Peter's was founded by his son C.M. Chavasse, who was later appointed Bishop of Rochester. Balliol College **(9)** was founded c. 1263 by John de Balliol, on the orders of the Bishop of Durham, as penance for Balliol's disagreements with the Church. Balliol's wife Devourguilla (who became patroness of the college after Balliol's death) was the great-granddaughter of David I of Scotland, as a result of which their son John reigned briefly as King of Scotland, from 1292-96. Jesus College **(10)** was founded in 1571 by Hugh Price, Treasurer of St David's cathedral in Wales, who persuaded Elizabeth I to add to the kudos of the college by allowing him to name her as founder.

E

scale 1:1,562.5

The Sheldonian Theatre **(1)** was designed by Christopher Wren, a former member of All Souls College **(10)** as a venue for degree ceremonies, and was funded by Gilbert Sheldon, Warden of All Souls, who was later appointed Archbishop of Canterbury. The Sheldonian, built from 1664–67, was also the original home of the Oxford University Press, which then moved to the Clarendon Building **(2)**, designed by Nicholas Hawksmoor and completed in 1715, before moving in 1830 to Walton Street (p. 8). The Old Ashmolean **(3)** was built from 1679–83 and, as the name suggests, was the original home of the Ashmolean Museum before it moved to Beaumont Street (p. 10); the building now houses the History of Science Museum. The Bodleian Library **(4)** was originally endowed in the 15th century by Duke Humphrey of Gloucester, younger brother of Henry V, and was first housed above the Divinity School **(5)**, the oldest part of which dates from the 1420s. From 1597–1602, Thomas Bodley, a Fellow of Merton College (p. 23) spent a vast amount of money restoring and extending the library, which reopened in 1602 as the Bodleian. The Bodleian is Britain's second largest library, with a collection of some six million books on more than 80 miles of shelves. The Radcliffe Camera **(6)** was designed by James Gibbs based on an idea conceived by Nicholas Hawksmoor and built from 1737–48 as the Radcliffe Library, funded by the bequest of John Radcliffe (see p. 9). It now serves as a reading room of the Bodleian Library. The colleges that surround this cornucopia of architecture include Exeter College **(7)**, Lincoln College **(8)**, founded in 1427 by Robert Fleming, Bishop of Lincoln, and Brasenose College **(9)**, founded in 1504 by Robert Smythe, another Bishop of Lincoln – the college stands on the site of the earlier Brasenose Hall, whose name is thought to derive from a 'brazen nose' gate-knocker that now hangs in the Hall. All Souls College **(10)** was co-founded in 1438 by Henry VI and Henry Chichele, Archbishop of Canterbury, as a memorial to soldiers killed in the Hundered Years' War, its full title being The College of All Souls of the Faithful Departed, of Oxford. Also to the west of Catte Street are Hertford College **(11)**, which includes the famous Bridge of Sighs, and New College **(12)** which belies its name at more then 600 years old, having been founded in 1379 by William of Wykeham, Bishop of Winchester. To the south of the High Street are Oriel College **(13)** and University College **(14)**, Oxford's oldest, founded by William, Bishop of Durham, in 1249. Oriel was founded in 1324 as St Mary's College by Adam de Brome, rector of St Mary the Virgin church, and refounded two years later by Edward II, after which it became known as King's College – the name Oriel comes from a house on this site named La Oriole, which was acquired by the college in 1329.

2 20

3

scale 1:1,562.5

Magdalen College **(1)** was founded in 1458 by William Waynflete, a graduate of New College **(2)** (and p. 19) and later Henry VI's Lord Chancellor. Because Magdalen was built outside the city walls (which stood to the west of Longwall Street, which runs north-south in the picture), there was plenty of space in which to build, making the college buildings more expansive than most: James I referred to it as 'the most absolute building in Oxford'. Magdalen's most famous feature is the Bell Tower, completed in 1505, from which the choristers sing madrigals in Latin at 6 a.m. on May Day, a tradition thought to have begun with the inauguration of the tower. Just inside the city walls, and far less spacious, is St Edmund Hall **(3)**, named in honour of St Edmund of Abingdon, Archbishop of Canterbury from 1234–40 and the last incumbent to be canonised. St. Edmund taught here c. 1195-1200, giving the Hall a claim to be Oxford's oldest teaching establishment, although it did not achieve full collegiate status until 1957. To the west of St Edmund Hall is Queen's College **(4)**, founded in 1341 by Robert de Eglesfield and named in honour of Queen Philippa (consort of Edward II), to whom Eglesfield was chaplain. The Examination Schools **(5)** were built from 1876–82 on the site of the Angel Inn, and are so named for the obvious reason that examinations were and still are held there; more recently, the schools have also been used for lectures and, outside term-time, for conferences.

Christ Church College **(1)** was originally founded in 1525 as Cardinal College by Cardinal Wolsey, and stands on the site of an 8th century nunnery dedicated to St Frideswide, whose buildings and church were incorporated in Wolsey's College. After the Cardinal's fall from favour and subsequent death (1529 and 1530 respectively), the college was refounded by Henry VIII in 1532, and then again in 1546, at which time the college was renamed Christ Church College – since then, Christ Church has been informally known as 'The House' from its Latin name, Aedes Christi. At the same time, the priory church was designated a cathedral **(2)** to serve the new diocese of Oxford – it is the smallest cathedral in England, but serves what is now the largest diocese. The college's impressive art collection is housed in Christ Church Picture Gallery **(3)**, designed by Powell and Moya, and built in 1968. On the other side of St Aldate's is Pembroke College **(4)**, founded in 1624 by Thomas Tesdale and Richard Wightwick, and named in honour of the 3rd Earl of Pembroke. Campion Hall **(5)**, to the south, is named after Roman Catholic martyr Edmund Campion, and is a Permanent Private Hall for Jesuit students. Corpus Christi College **(6)** was founded in 1517 by Robert Foxe, who became Lord Privy Seal to Henrys VII and VIII, and who likened the college he founded to a beehive, hoping that **'the scholars night and day may make wax and sweet honey to the honour of God, and the advantage of themselves and all Christian men'**. Merton College **(7)** was founded in 1264 by Walter de Merton (later Bishop of Rochester) in Malden, Surrey. The college moved to Oxford about a decade later, where the college and its statutes, dated 1274, became the model for the collegiate system at both Oxford and Cambridge. The Music Faculty Building **(8)** was built in 1936 and is now the home of the Bate Collection, an extensive collection of musical instruments including a harpsichord played by Handel.

3

C   D   E

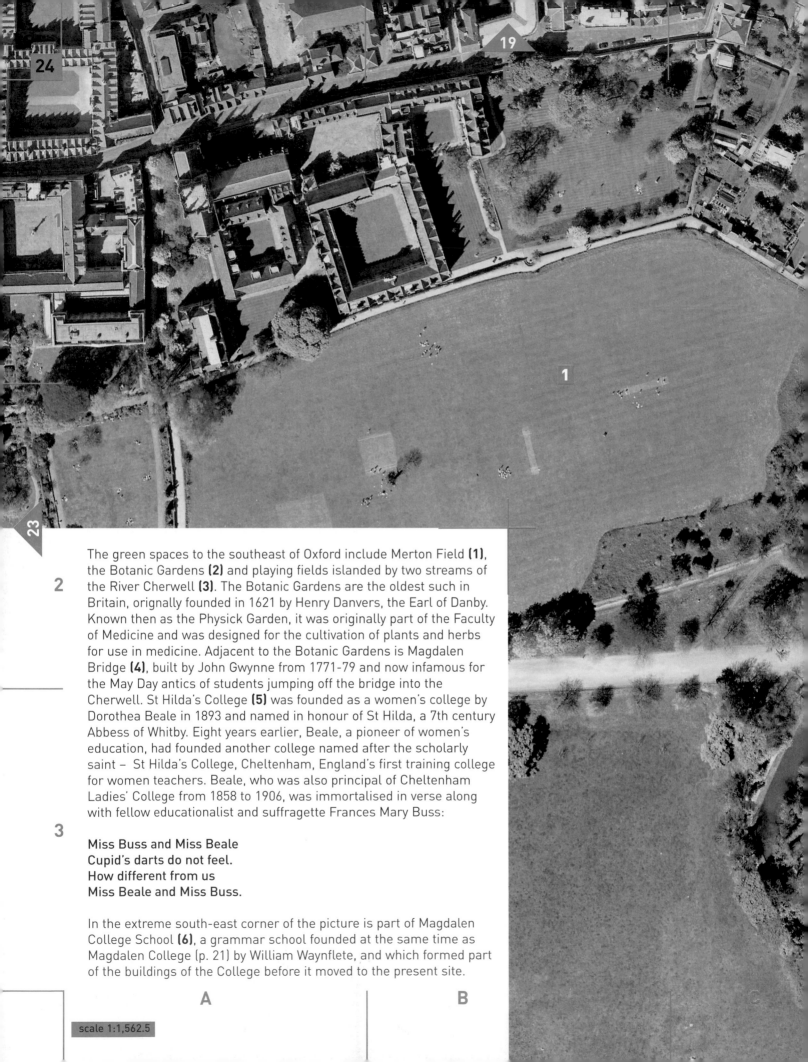

1

2

The green spaces to the southeast of Oxford include Merton Field **(1)**, the Botanic Gardens **(2)** and playing fields islanded by two streams of the River Cherwell **(3)**. The Botanic Gardens are the oldest such in Britain, orignally founded in 1621 by Henry Danvers, the Earl of Danby. Known then as the Physick Garden, it was originally part of the Faculty of Medicine and was designed for the cultivation of plants and herbs for use in medicine. Adjacent to the Botanic Gardens is Magdalen Bridge **(4)**, built by John Gwynne from 1771-79 and now infamous for the May Day antics of students jumping off the bridge into the Cherwell. St Hilda's College **(5)** was founded as a women's college by Dorothea Beale in 1893 and named in honour of St Hilda, a 7th century Abbess of Whitby. Eight years earlier, Beale, a pioneer of women's education, had founded another college named after the scholarly saint – St Hilda's College, Cheltenham, England's first training college for women teachers. Beale, who was also principal of Cheltenham Ladies' College from 1858 to 1906, was immortalised in verse along with fellow educationalist and suffragette Frances Mary Buss:

3

Miss Buss and Miss Beale
Cupid's darts do not feel.
How different from us
Miss Beale and Miss Buss.

In the extreme south-east corner of the picture is part of Magdalen College School **(6)**, a grammar school founded at the same time as Magdalen College (p. 21) by William Waynflete, and which formed part of the buildings of the College before it moved to the present site.

A

B

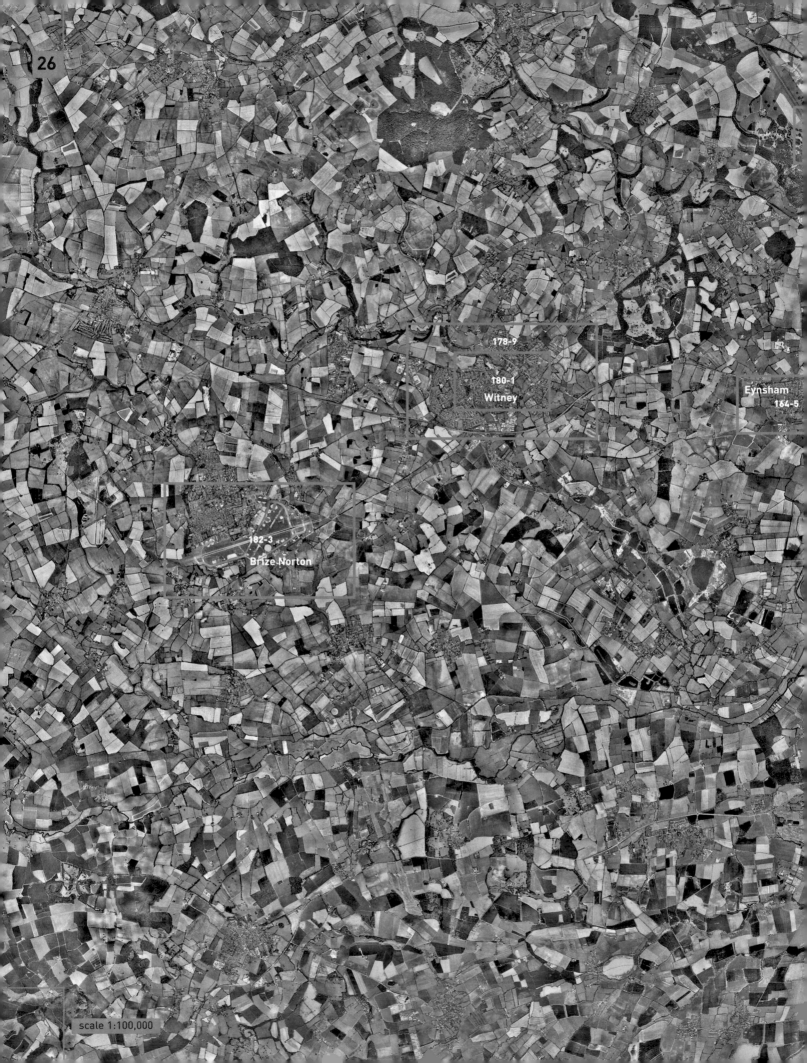

26

178-9

180-1
Witney

Eynsham
164-5

182-3
Brize Norton

scale 1:100,000

172-3
Woodstock
-5
enheim Palace
Oxford Airport
172-3

166-7
Kidlington

Gosford

168-9 170-1

Yarnton

28-29
Cutteslowe

Wolvercote
30-31 32-33 34-35

Wytham 38-39 40-41 42-43 44-45
36-37 Summertown Marston

46-47 48-49 50-51 52-53 54-55 56-57
Sandhills

60-61 62-63 64-65 66-67 68-69 70-71
Headington

58-59

Jericho
72-73 74-75 76-77 78-79 80-81
O X F O R D

82-83
Shotover 152-3
Wheatley

84-85 86-87 88-89 90-91 92-93 94-95 96-97
Botley Osney

102-3 104-5 106-7 108-9
Horspath
98-99 100-1 118-119
Cumnor New Hinksey
110-11 112-13 114-15 116-17
Cowley

Iffley
120-1 122-3 124-5 126-7 128-9

130-1

132-3 134-5 136-7
Littlemoor

Boar's Hill 142-3 144-5
138-9 140-1 Kennington
Sandford 150-1
Wootton 146-7 148-9

154-5
Northcourt

156-7 158-9

A B I N G D O N
162-3

160-1

oxford canal/a34-a44 interchange/pear tree service area/pear tree park & ride/linkside lake

1

3

28

31

E

32

E

37

32

28

31

scale 1:3,125

29

33

34

39

banbury road/sunnymead

34

29

33

scale 1:3,125

40

38

32

37

46

scale 1:3,125

39

scale 1:3,125

41 2

43

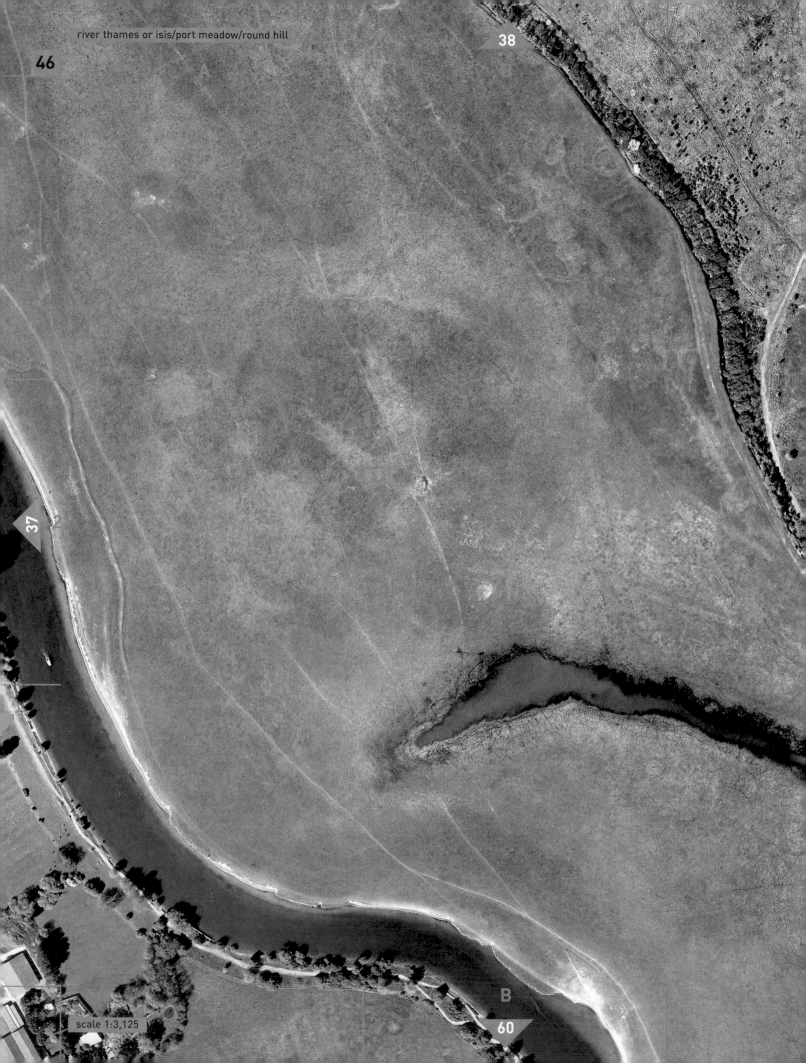

46

38

37 2

B

60

scale 1:3,125

oxford canal/aristotle bridge

48

40

47

B

62

scale 1:3,125

41

49

50

63

50

42

49

64

scale 1:6,250

43

51

52

65

B

C

51

B

53

68

58

36

A

B

84

85

37

marley wood plantation/a34 western by-pass/wytham or seacourt stream/a34-a420 interchange/botley bridge/seacourt park & ride

59

60

72

scale 1:3,125

47

61

62

73

62

48

61

scale 1:3,125

74

63

66

52

65

78

scale 1:3,125

68

54

67

80

scale 1:3,125

55

69

70

81

70

56

69

82

scale 1:3,125

botley stream/bulstake stream

72

60

1

59

scale 1:3,125

88

73

scale 1:3,125

78

82

71

81

97

118

scale 1:6,250

red house farm/noble's farm cottages/tudor court park/a420 cumnor hill by-pass

A

B

2

scale 1:3,125

a420 cumnor hill by-pass/dean court

58

99

98

b4044 eynsham road west/botley

A

85

B

scale 1:3,125

100

88

72

87

101

scale 1:3,125

90

74

89

3

102

scale 1:3,125

75
91
92
103

91

scale 1:3,125

scale 1:3,125

96

95

scale 1:3,125

99

2

3

B

121

scale 1:6,250

north hinksey village/hinksey stream/a34 southern by-pass/harcourt hill/hinksey heights golf course

grandpont/cricket ground/sports ground/hinksey stream

102

90

101

110

scale 1:3,125

91

104

111

cowley road

106

94

105

114

scale 1:3,125

107

1

2

97

b4495 hollow way

109

118

117

101

railway sidings/new hinksey/hinksey stream/cold harbour

university college sports ground/river thames or isis/long bridges bathing place/weirs mill stream

111

scale 1:3,125

114

113

scale 1:3,125

116

108

115

scale 1:3,125

128

118

82

109

117

130

3

whitebarn/henwod farm/youlbury wood

120

99

138

B

C

A

B

C

1

2

3

A

scale 1:6,250

122

101

121

140

scale 1:6,250

110

123

124

132

141

124

112

B

123

scale 1:3,125

132

B

113

125

126

133

126

114

125

134

scale 1:3,125

128

116

127

136

scale 1:3,125

scale 1:6,250

132

124

123

142

a423 by-pass road/river thames or isis/sewage works/heyford hill roundabout

134

126

133

144

scale 1:3,125

136

128

135

150

scale 1:3,125

130

scale 1:6,250

E

139

A

C

141

144

scale 1:3,125

135

145

150

149

146

142

141

scale 1:3,125

148

144

147

sewage works/oxford united (new ground)/blackbird leys

136/7

scale 1:6,250

littleworth/wheatley/a40

152

A

B

C

B

scale 1:6,250

C

D

E

3

156

154

160

scale 1:6,250

157

scale 1:6,250

abingdon

162

157

156

161

scale 1:3,125

157

158

161

D

D

E

B

C

B

169

scale 1:6,250

campsfield/a34/oxford airport

172

175

scale 1:6,250

174

1

B

C

2

174

174

2

3

174

174

A

B

C

B

C

scale 1:3,125

C

D

2

3

C

D

E

scale 1:6,250

A

C

C

D

E

index

The index reads in the sequence: street name / page number / grid reference. A grid reference is given to all streets found within the pages of cartography.